This book is dedicated to our mother,
Frieda Grotrian Augenstein.
Mom had an amazing "green thumb" and could
make anything grow and thrive. Growing up, we
were surrounded by gorgeous flower gardens filled
with many varieties of flowers. Mom instilled a love
of gardening in us; especially *flower* gardening.

Thanks Mom.

Gloria and Jeanette

ABOUT THE AUTHORS

Gloria Doty is a freelance writer, author, speaker and blogger. Her work has been published in magazines, devotionals and anthologies. She is a contributing writer for *Hope-Full Living*, a devotional for seniors. She is the author of the book, *Not Different Enough*, about her daughter's life with autism, Asperger's and intellectual disabilities.

Gloria is a mother, grandmother and great-grandmother. She resides in Fort Wayne, IN and is a member of St. Michael Lutheran Church.

Jeanette Dall is a freelance writer and author living in Batavia, IL. Her work has been published by national educational and Christian publishers. She is the co-author of *God and Me* and *Gotta Have God* for children, she was a contributing writer for *The Amazing Bible Factbook* and *Extreme Bible Facts* and currently writes devotions for *Hope-Full Living,* a devotional for seniors.

Jeanette is a mother and grandmother and is a member of Immanuel Lutheran Church.

ACKNOWLEDGEMENTS

Thank you to...

...a friend and dedicated photographer, Ida M. Smith-Kaiser, of Smith-Kaiser-Images, for many of the photos contained in this book

...Cheryll Iddings of CAIddings Photography for sharing her photos

...morguefile.com for images

...Julie Stuckey and Stuckey's Greenhouse, 1919 Tyler Avenue, Fort Wayne, IN for graciously allowing us to photograph the many beautiful flowers available there

...Lynnell Detraz for sharing her beautiful orchids and her knowledge of orchids

...Shirley Burgess for her continual encouragement

All images were used with permission.

AFRICAN DAISY

African Daisies are grown primarily for their bright, cheerful, daisy-like flower heads and due to their brightness are referred to as the Goddess of the Sun.

BLOOM WHERE YOU ARE PLANTED

The words in the title are a common saying about people, but in the case of the african daisy, it applies to the flower. This bright flower *prefers* a spot in warm, sunny, rich soil but it will *tolerate* drought, shade and poor soil. The blooms may not be as plentiful nor as large, but it will survive.

Can we say that about our lives? We have all kinds of things and conditions we *prefer* in our lives. I prefer to be employed, have a nice car and good health. However, sometimes plans don't work out the way I *prefer*.

Conditions in my life may not be perfect but if I trust in God to be with me, I can *tolerate* a lot of conditions. Jesus died for me and you and if we believe that, with his help, we will survive all circumstances. It is called contentment. Paul wrote about it in his letter to the Philippians:

I have learned to be content whatever the circumstances. I know what it is to be in need and I know what it is to have plenty. I have learned the secret of being content in any and every situation, whether well fed or hungry, whether living in plenty or in want.
Philippians 4:11-12

BEGONIA

Begonias are native to tropical and subtropical areas, mostly occurring in South and Central America and Asia.

DEFINITION, PLEASE

Describing what makes a begonia, a begonia, is a bit difficult. They can be evergreen or deciduous. Some are climbers, some are shrubs and some are trailers, while others are succulents. Some varieties have roots, some have rhizomes and still others are tuberous.

There are begonias that thrive in moist, rainforest conditions, while others tolerate drier climates. They can be annuals or perennials depending on the variety.

If most people were asked, "What makes a christian, a christian?" there would be as many differing answers as there are about begonias. Unfortunately, even many christians can't always answer that question. There are individuals who believe a certain denomination is the defining factor.

The person who accepts Jesus Christ as the son of God and as their personal Savior and believes he died and rose again for them is a christian.

Just as there are many types of begonias, there are many types of people. All the varieties are still called begonias; not all people can be called christians.

Yet to all who did receive him, to those who believed in his name, he gave the right to become children of God.
John1:12

IMPATIENS

Impatiens are the symbol of motherly love. In medieval times, they were used in gardens devoted to the Virgin Mary, the mother symbol of the christian world.

DAILY WATERING

Impatiens became popular in the United States in the 1950s and have remained an extremely popular flower for home gardeners. Part of their popularity can be attributed to the many choices of available colors. There are several varieties, some with single blossoms and some with double blossoms.

They are easy to plant and are relatively free from disease and pests. Impatiens do have shallow root systems, however. This requires shade conditions and daily watering if they are to remain beautiful. I remember thinking after a particularly heavy downpour, I wouldn't have to water my planters of impatiens for a few days. I was wrong. Within one day, the plants were severely drooping. The good thing is once they received the needed moisture, they immediately returned to their blooming grandeur.

Many times, we think an occasional 'drink' of God's word is sufficient for us for the next few weeks or months.

We need a *daily* 'watering' of God's word to keep us spiritually healthy. When we are in the midst of a drought, we begin to droop. Thankfully, just as with the impatiens, we can be revived by refreshing ourselves with daily bible reading, prayers and worship.

For day after day they seek me out; they seem eager to know my ways…
Isaiah 58:2

LILAC

The Arnold Arboretum claims America's oldest lilacs are believed to be in Portsmouth, NH, where they were planted at the home of Governor Benning Wentworth more than 250 years ago.

OUT OF REACH

Gardeners have long prized lilacs, not only for their beauty and heady fragrance, but because they are 'survivors.' They can survive in many different climates. That was one of the reasons pioneer families dug up their lilac bushes and took them West with them; they were certain they could survive no matter what kind of climate they would find in their new homes. Those transplants did survive and lilacs can be found across the country.

There are new varieties which grow much closer to the ground, but the older varieties grow quite tall, which means all the beautiful flowers are at the top of the bush and out of reach. You would need a stepladder to pick some for a bouquet.

There are times when Christians appear similar to the lilacs. The outside world, the skeptics and the unbelievers, often see believers as lofty and 'out of reach.' They don't think we can understand their world, their problems or their pain. That is the exact opposite of what Christ taught us to do.

He associated with the sick, the outcasts and the lowly. Isn't that our mission, also? We need to bring the fragrance of God's love and salvation down to a level that others can see and enjoy.

[15] For we are to God the pleasing aroma of Christ among those who are being saved and those who are perishing.
2 Corinthians 2:15

PHLOX

Phlox is a Greek word meaning 'flame.' The name was most likely chosen due to the bright, vivid colors of these plants.

TOGETHER IS BETTER

The phlox flower originally came from North America and was available in England by the early 1800s. It quickly grew in popularity and is still found in gardens across the country. Two of the varieties are named after famous painters: Rembrandt and Van Gogh. These lovely flowers have a sweet fragrance and are easily grown.

There are many varieties of these beautiful flowers, ranging in height from the tall, 3-4 ft plants to the ground-huggers, known as 'creeping phlox.'

The most commonly recognized phlox have large heads of flowers on strong stems. Each of these heads is comprised of many small, individual blossoms, perfectly shaped with a star in the center. If each flower was divided into the individual blossoms, it would not be attractive or useful for arrangements.

The same is true of people. We can be used by God as individuals but think of the unique opportunities we have to pool our usefulness when we join with others. We can make a bigger difference in advancing God's kingdom and telling others of his love if we work together.

[24] And let us consider how we may spur one another on toward love and good deeds, [25] not giving up meeting together, as some are in the habit of doing, but encouraging one another—and all the more as you see the Day approaching.
Hebrews 10:24-25

CHRISTMAS CACTUS

The stems of the Christmas Cactus consist of small cushiony sections called "areoles." On other cacti, spines and true leaves arise from the areoles. The flowers on the holiday cactus are formed on the tips of the segments.

CHOOSE YOUR BLOOM TIME

A Christmas cactus makes a wonderful gift for anyone who likes flowers. It is unique and beautiful and definitely a conversation piece.

This cactus is also a study in contradictions. When we think of cacti, our minds automatically picture dry, hot, sun-filled, desert-like conditions. In reality, the Christmas cactus likes many daily hours of darkness, its desired temperature is 68 degrees F. and for optimum blooming, it should be 'misted' every day, rather than watered.

My 'Christmas' cactus blooms at Thanksgiving, Christmas, Easter and occasionally, in the summer. No one told it when it was *supposed* to bloom. Perhaps we should be more like my cactus. I have heard people say they are too old, too young, too disabled, too forgetful or too tired to work in God's kingdom any longer. Just because our mind pictures one thing, doesn't mean it is necessarily true. There are no *supposed to* times in our lives; we can *bloom* at any time.

The Christmas cactus can live for 20-30 years and produce blooms along the way. We have God-given talents and abilities we can share at any time of our lives. Our gifts may change, but our need to tell others of Jesus' death and resurrection for us, never changes.

Many are the plans in a person's heart, but it is the LORD's
purpose that prevails.
Proverbs 19:21

SNAPDRAGON

The English name derives from the flower's imagined appearance as a dragon's face. The variety is loved by children, who delight in squeezing the sides of the flower to see the 'dragon's mouth' open and close or 'snap' shut.

CHANGE YOUR FAMILY?

As a child, I delighted in picking some of the individual blossoms off the snapdragon plants growing in my mother's garden. I would pinch the sides and the 'mouth' would open. Occasionally, I would have one in each hand and my little dragons would have conversations with each other.

These interesting flowers come in a variety of sizes; small, dwarf plants to medium and very tall plants. They happily reseed themselves and you may find them in places you didn't plant them as the birds like to carry the seeds. They are classified as annuals; however, I live in a very cold winter climate and still, they reappear every year.

As I researched the snapdragon, I discovered they were in one specific botanical family for many years. Then botanists, studying the plant's DNA, decided they were really not of that particular species and genus, but part of an entirely different family. So they were moved.

Isn't it a comfort to know we may be from different cultures and experiences, but if we are in God's family, we are there to stay? If we accept Jesus Christ as our Savior and believe he died and rose again, for *us*, we can't suddenly be moved to another family, regardless of our DNA.

12 Yet to all who did receive him, to those who believed in his name, he gave the right to become children of God.
John 1:12

AMARYLLIS

The word amaryllis comes from the Greek word "amaryssein" which means 'to sparkle.' Amaryllis is also known as belladonna lily or March lily due to its propensity to flower around March. It is a native of the Western Cape region of South Africa.

SACRIFICE and REQUIREMENTS

Often, amaryllis bulbs are given as gifts. They are in a box, already planted in a pot containing the perfect soil. The only thing *required* of the person receiving the gift is to remove it from the box, water the bulb minimally and wait 7-10 weeks for huge, glorious blooms to appear. Those trumpet-shaped blooms are on 2 - 3 foot stalks. The flowers are red, bright pink and orange with leaves measuring 18 inches long and 1 1/2 inches wide. Some of the blooms measure 12" across.

In Greek mythology, Amaryllis was the name of a shepherdess who loved a conceited shepherd. The shepherd *required* her to create a flower in order to receive his love. In return, she made the ultimate sacrifice by piercing herself in the heart to create a beautiful red blossom.

By God's grace, we are not *required* to *do* anything to gain his love. It is a gift; all we have to do is accept it, unwrap it, and enjoy it. Jesus *sacrificed* himself so we may have the free gift of forgiveness and eternal salvation. If we accept him as our Lord and Savior, the requirements are met for us.

For the wages of sin is death, but the gift of God is eternal life in Christ Jesus our Lord.
Romans 6:23

ORCHID

Orchids are one of the oldest and largest families of plants in the world. They inhabit every corner of the planet with the exception of the driest deserts and Antarctica. More than 17,000 species are known, with countless varieties in size and shape.

TOO DIFFICULT

The beautiful colors, varied shapes and delicate scents, plus the fact they don't grow in soil but in air, makes orchids seem almost magical. The majority of flower lovers are mesmerized by orchids; however, orchids have the reputation of being temperamental, requiring too much care and being entirely too difficult. That is probably the reason most people are reluctant to try raising one. In reality, orchids are neither difficult nor fragile plants; some are nearly indestructible.

My friend has a sunroom filled with gorgeous orchids. She has many types and varieties; all thriving and healthy. To have an orchid thrive, as she does, she needed to learn some facts and inform herself about their care.

Occasionally, our lives seem too difficult to manage. We feel as though relationships, especially our relationship with our heavenly Father, are much too complicated. Perhaps, as with orchids, we need to learn more and continue to grow in knowledge in order to maintain a healthy God relationship. We should never stop seeking godly knowledge and be willing to grow and bloom. Reading God's word, listening to teachers, communicating with fellow believers and spending time in prayer are great ways to learn and grow. We can then be indestructible instead of fragile and difficult.

[16] Let the message of Christ dwell among you richly as you teach and admonish one another with all wisdom through psalms, hymns, and songs from the Spirit, singing to God with gratitude in your hearts.
Colossians 3:16

HOLLYHOCK

A hollyhock flower, known in Japan as aoi was incorporated into an official seal in Japan, and has maintained importance in modern Japanese culture. It inspired the name and symbol of a Japanese professional soccer club and the Hollyhock Festival is one of the three main festivals of the city of Kyoto.

SUPPORT

Hollyhocks are popular garden ornamental plants. They are easily grown from seed and the red-hued flowers attract hummingbirds and butterflies. Many children have enjoyed using the flowers and buds to make hollyhock *dolls* in fancy dresses.

Due to the hollyhock's height of 6-9 feet; a strong wind or the weight of water in the blossoms and on the leaves after a heavy rain can cause the stalks to bend and break if they aren't supported. They need to be tied to stakes or a fence to stay upright.

Our lives are much the same. The strong winds of doubt and fear can cause us to bend and break. When worries and problems 'rain' down on us, the weight can be more than we can bear. We become bent over and feel as though we will break, just like the stalks of the hollyhock.

We need support, also. We need the support of friends who encourage us and hold us up during the hard circumstances of life. We need the support found in God's word and daily prayer.

If we remember how much God loves us: enough to send his son to die for us, and we have *fastened* ourselves to him and his word, his support will keep us upright.

So do not fear, for I am with you; do not be dismayed, for I am your God. I will strengthen you and help you; I will uphold you with my righteous right hand.
Isaiah 41:10

POPPY

The red poppies have been associated with war since the Napoleonic Wars when a writer of that time first noted how the poppies grew over the graves of soldiers. The damage done to the landscape in Flanders during the battle in WW1 greatly increased the lime content in the soil, leaving the poppy as one of the few plants able to grow in the region.

SYMBOLS FOR REMEMBERING

When I was a child, I remember shopping with my mother when a person would be selling red paper poppies outside the store. Mom always bought a few but no one ever told me what they represented and I guess I didn't ask.

I later learned the poppies were sold in November before Remembrance Day (also known as Poppy Day or Armistice Day) as a memorial day observed in Commonwealth countries since the end of World War I. The red flower represents the battlefields saturated with blood, and the men and women who fought bravely in times of war.

People wear all sorts of symbols; some represent positive things and some purposely represent negative ideas. When we see the symbol of a poppy or the actual flower, we remember the *many* lives sacrificed for freedom; freedom from human tyrants who want(ed) complete rule of this world.

When we wear a cross symbol, whether it is on our clothing, our jewelry or even as a tattoo, we are remembering the *ONE* life sacrificed for all mankind and the blood spilled for *our* freedom; freedom from the tyrants of sin, death and the devil, who also wants complete rule of the world.

And I will make every effort to see that after my departure
you will always be able to remember these things.
2 Peter 1:15

HYACINTH

Hyacinths have been cultivated commercially since the second half of the 16th century. They became very popular in 18th and early 19th century Europe.

SWEET AROMA

The hyacinth is known not only for its beautiful vibrant colors but also for the unmistakable aroma. If a few are cut and placed in a vase, a person can smell the fragrance as soon as they walk in the room. It permeates an entire area of the house.

There are several Greek myths of the origin of the hyacinth, but the truth is God knew when he created it we needed this bloom for several of our senses. The individual star-shaped florets combine on a stem to make a compact mini-bush of pink, blue, white, orchid or salmon. It is a delight for our eyes and a blessing for our sense of smell.

God knew what he was doing when he created us, too. How do we appear to other believers and to unbelievers? Are our lives and actions God-pleasing when others see us? Do we leave a lovely aroma with strangers or do they wrinkle their noses at our 'stink?'

Perhaps we should remember the short little hyacinth. It isn't tall and strong like some flowers; it doesn't climb a trellis or spread out over a large area. It simply pushes up through the ground in the spring and delights everyone who is fortunate enough to be near. Wouldn't it be wonderful if others thought they were blessed to be near us?

For we are to God the aroma of Christ among those who are being saved and those who are perishing. To the one we are the smell of death; to the other the fragrance of life.
2 Corinthians 2: 15, 16

CHRYSANTHEMUM

The Chinese named their royal throne after the chrysanthemum and the Japanese Imperial family uses a Chrysanthemum Seal as the imperial seal of Japan. Japan celebrates the chrysanthemum in a national festival held annually in September. Chrysanthemum flowers are used to make chrysanthemum tea in China.

REMOVING THE FADED

The name "chrysanthemum" is derived from the Greek words *chrysos* (gold) and *anthemon* (flower). These plants are commonly referred to simply as 'mums' and even though they are a very common flower and nearly every home garden has a few, they have quite a long list of credentials associated with them.

In Japan, the 'Festival of Happiness' celebrates the flower. The chrysanthemum is the official flower of Chicago, Illinois and Salinas, California. A certain species of yellow or white chrysanthemum flowers can be boiled to make tea. A rice wine flavored with the flowers is made in Korea. The plants have even been shown to reduce indoor air pollution.

Knowing all these facts will not help your plant be vigorous and beautiful. To accomplish that, every garden book will instruct you to remove the faded blooms.

Do we have faded blooms in our lives? Old hurts, jealousies and actions that need forgiveness? Worries, stress? Those things are like faded blossoms; they need to be cut off and thrown away. It isn't a one-time job; it is a *daily* task. If we ask God to help us remove these things from our lives, it will provide the opportunity for us to thrive and continue to bloom.

Being confident of this, that he who began a good work in you will carry it on to completion until the day of Christ Jesus.
Philippians 1:6

LANTANA

If you have a hot, baked-by-the-sun, spot in your yard, lantana is your answer. This hardworking plant not only thrives with little moisture and in full, unyielding sun, it does so with ease.

AKIN TO TEMPTATIONS

The lantana plant seems to 'have it all.' It thrives in the heat, it requires little moisture, the blooms are showy and bright, it attracts butterflies and hummingbirds and is easily spread by song birds dropping the seeds.

When a plant has so many good qualities, it is difficult to think of it possibly having a 'dark side.' But it does. In regions where it is planted as a groundcover, it can quickly become invasive and take over. All parts of this beautiful plant, from leaves and stems to blossoms, are toxic and can be lethal if ingested in quantity.

So many things in our lives are closely related to this plant and its description. Most temptations that come our way aren't ugly or repulsive; they are beautiful and we convince ourselves of the good qualities of our 'desires.' Many times, we discover the dark, poisonous side of our pleasure when it is too late. If we continue in our consumption, it can be lethal to our body and also to our soul.

Fortunately, we have the antidote. Jesus Christ died *for* us, so when we ask for forgiveness and for help in resisting the temptations which come our way, he is always there to forgive and give us strength.

Have mercy on me, O God, according to your unfailing love; according to your great compassion, blot out my transgressions. Wash away all my iniquity and cleanse me from my sin.
Psalm 51: 1,2

PENTAS

The dark green foliage of penta plants is slightly fuzzy, and the five-petaled blossoms grow in 3-inch clusters similar to other butterfly favorites like sedum, lantana, and Queen Anne's lace. Colors include pink, purple, white, and red.

NEEDING THE LIGHT

The scientific name for penta comes from a word meaning 'five' indicating the number of petals on the flowers. These star-like petals grow in clusters which attract hummingbirds and especially, butterflies. The butterflies continuously take nectar from dawn to dusk every day during their long blooming season.

You can purchase plants or you can start your pentas from seed. Unlike other seeds which are covered with a layer of soil when planted, these seeds need light to germinate so they are placed on top of the soil and must not be covered.

We need the light of God's love and grace to shine on us. Our lives are often covered with the dirt of doubts, worries, fears and sins. These things tend to bury us and cause us to struggle to push through all the adversity. If we ask for forgiveness, the 'soil' is pushed back and we can flourish as we bask in the light of God's love.

Then we can be a blessing to others and provide spiritual nourishment just as the pentas provide nectar to the butterflies.

But I have raised you up for this very purpose, that I might show you my power and that my name might be proclaimed in all the earth.
Exodus 9:16

COSMOS

The word cosmos is derived from the Greek, which means a balanced universe.

FAMILY

As I researched the cosmos flower, I discovered they are in the same family as sunflowers, daisies and asters. Although these 'family members' may have some of the same botanical characteristics, they certainly do not look alike. Their foliage is different, their colors vary, their growth is different and their susceptibilities to pests are all things which set them apart from each other. Their seeds are especially different as the seeds of the cosmos look like pine needles.

The people in God's family are certainly different, also. Besides the obvious differences of age, height, race, skin color and gender, there are the differences in preferences to consider. Some prefer contemporary services while others like traditional. Some people prefer one version of the bible over another version.

Rather than concentrating on the differences, we should put more energy into seeing the likenesses. Just as in the flower world, a 'family' of flowers has a long list of similarities or the experts would not put them together. They may look different but they are all beautiful.

We belong to God's family. If we accept Jesus as our savior and the true son of God, the differences aren't nearly as important as the fact we are his children. We may all look different but we can each bloom in this world, in our own way.

See what great love the Father has lavished on us, that we should be called children of God! And that is what we are!
1 John 3:1

BLACK-EYED SUSAN

There are several theories about the origin of the name for this hardy perennial. 'Black-Eyed Susan' is the title of a poem written by John Gay, (1685-1732) a poet from the pre-Elizabethan era. Regardless of where the name originated, the black-eyed susan is a flower which can be found in all fifty states and across Canada. It is one of the most popular wildflowers grown.

PIONEER FLOWER

This prolific flower has many 'claims to fame.' It is the state flower of Maryland and as such, the Preakness horse race, run each year in Baltimore, is known as the Run for the Black-Eyed Susans. It was used extensively by many Native American tribes as a medicinal plant. Perhaps the most descriptive nickname for it is the Pioneer Flower.

It doesn't signify its use by the pioneers, but rather the fact it is one of the first plants to reappear after a disaster, such as a forest fire. It lifts its golden yellow head out of the ruins and blooms again.

Shouldn't we be like the black-eyed susan? Disasters come in many forms; natural disasters, personal disasters, emotional disasters and relational disasters. It is difficult to lift our heads and have the strength to survive. God understands and is there to help us, encourage us and give us the strength to 'live again.' If a disaster has been experienced by a friend, acquaintance or an entire region of the country, we should strive to help them *re-bloom*.

Think of a time when God helped you survive and bloom again after a disaster.

Have mercy on me, Oh God, have mercy on me, for in you my souls takes refuge. I will take refuge in the shadow of your wings until the disaster has passed.
Psalm 57:1

COLUMBINE

Aquilegia common names: Granny's Bonnet or Columbine, are perennial plants found in meadows, woodlands and at higher altitudes throughout the Northern Hemisphere. These flowers are known for the spurred petals of their flowers.

HAWKS AND DOVES

The genus name *Aquilegia* is derived from the Latin word for eagle (*aquila*), due to the shape of the flower petals, which are said to resemble an eagle's claw. The common name "columbine" comes from the Latin for "dove", due to the resemblance of the inverted flower to five doves clustered together.

The words eagle and dove seem to be on opposite ends of the spectrum. When we think of an eagle, we envision power, majesty, fierceness and protection. The word dove brings images of quiet gentleness, meekness, a soft countenance. It doesn't seem as though they should be descriptions of the same flower and yet, they are.

When we try to describe our heavenly father, we have the same problem. God tells us he is a fierce protector of his children; willing and able to defend us against all enemies. He offered his son to die for us so we can spend eternity with him.

He is also our loving, gentle father who invites us to crawl into his lap and tell him our problems. His word soothes us, calms us and takes away our fears.

So do not fear, for I am with you; do not be dismayed, for I am your God. I will strengthen you and help you; I will uphold you with my righteous right hand.
Psalm 41:10

SPIDER FLOWER

The Spider Plant is originally from southern Brazil, Paraguay and northern Argentina. In the United States, it has long been associated with President Thomas Jefferson's garden at Monticello.

RESEEDING

Cleome, or spider flower, is an annual known for its exceedingly long seedpods. The seedpods develop below the flowers as blooms progress upward on the stalk. Those seedpods and the extra long stamens give the plants a spidery look; hence the name, spider plant.

My mother always had a large bed of these beautiful plants. I didn't know the difference between an annual and a perennial, but they were there every year and I never saw my mother plant them. Even though they are an annual and die each fall in cold climates, they are prolific at reseeding themselves. The seedpods shatter easily and the many seeds fall to the ground, waiting for the spring sunshine.

Do we reseed ourselves? The majority of people have children, so the answer would be 'yes.' But the bigger question is, do we take the time to let the 'seeds' of our faith in Jesus Christ and our love for him 'fall' onto the next generation? Do we tell our children and grandchildren all the ways God has blessed us?

Even when I am old and gray, do not forsake me, my God, till I declare your power to the next generation, your mighty acts to all who are to come.
Psalm 71:18

CONEFLOWER

The coneflower is a native North American perennial. It has daisy-like flowers with raised centers. The flower, plant, and root of some types are used in herbal remedies.

ALMOST PERFECT

When reading through the many attributes of the coneflower, I thought it was nearly perfect. It is an easy to grow perennial and comes back each year. It is a low maintenance, fast-growing plant which produces an abundance of blooms in a variety of colors.

The coneflower can be grown in full sun. It thrives in summer's heat, doesn't mind drought and tolerates winter's cold. Butterflies love the nectar, songbirds are attracted to it for the seeds and the deer *won't* nibble on it. The flower, plant and root are used in herbal remedies. It seems like the absolute perfect flower.

But nothing is perfect. The coneflower does need to be well drained, the stems tend to bend and fall over after a bit of wind and the bright colors fade.

Sometimes we, as christians, like to show ourselves as nearly perfect, also. We don't want the world to see our faults, inferiorities, fears and shortcomings. However, if we are perfect, we have no need of God's love or forgiveness, purchased with the very blood of Jesus.

It is better for the world to see our love and trust in God which takes our fears and frailties and uses them for his purpose. We aren't perfect; we are forgiven.

For the law appoints as high priests men in all their weakness; but the oath, which came after the law, appointed the Son, who has been made perfect forever.
Hebrews 7: 28

CLEMATIS

The clematis is called the 'aristocrat of climbers' and 'queen of the vines.' The name clematis comes from the Greek word for vine. There are 297 species of clematis, including a few bush varieties. The clematis is not without its dark side. All parts of the plant are toxic, creating a severe burning sensation if eaten.

RESURRECTION FLOWER

I purchased a clematis plant a few years ago, with no knowledge of its requirements. It was fall and I was eager to get it planted before winter; however, I couldn't decide where its permanent home should be, so I put it in a deck planter.

In the spring, I transplanted it next to my garage. It was a shady spot, close to the foundation and not a very deep hole. I learned clematis should be planted fairly deep, they require lots of sunlight and should definitely not be next to a foundation. I was also told I should have pruned it in the fall.

The next spring, all I saw was the hard, dried, twisted, totally dead-looking vines. A few days later, I noticed a few small green leaves on the bottom of the trunk. Each day, there were more, until it was a huge green bush covered in beautiful purple blossoms.

Probably no one but me has ever called a clematis a resurrection flower, but that is what I think of each spring when I see the miraculous recovery from brittle dead vines to luxuriant growth and blooms.

Even though we do all the incorrect things, God brings us back from the dead and dormancy of our sinful lives into new life in Christ, if we accept him as our savior. We can be beautiful bloomers, too.

Jesus said to her, "I am the resurrection and the life. He who believes in me will live, even though he dies."
John 11:25

GERANIUM

There are over 400 known species of geraniums. Gardeners treasure them for both their flowers and foliage.

POSITIVES AND NEGATIVES

Geraniums are easily grown, like full sun and are known for their attractive leaves and bright-colored flowers that bloom throughout the growing season. You can plant these flowers in garden beds, hanging pots or window boxes. They come in a variety of sizes and shapes. The single, double or semi-double flowers come in nearly every color from purple to orange, red, white and lavender -- sometimes two colors. Many have scents as well: peppermint, lemon, orange, pineapple, nutmeg, rose or lime.

These plants have their fair share of problems. Pests include spider mites, thrips, mealybugs, slugs and caterpillars. Leaf spots may become problems in cool, wet weather, causing wilting. Grey mold and mildew may also become a problem.

Isn't that an accurate description of our lives, as well? We can list our positive qualities; our spiritual gifts, our giving and our volunteering of time and talents. All of these are God-pleasing virtues. However, like the geranium, we humans have our fair share of problems, also. Satan is ever-attacking with the thrips, mealybugs, mildew and slugs of daily life. Just as the geranium needs the gardener's help to become a beautiful, healthy flower, *we* need God's help to resist and avoid the negatives in our lives so we can mature and grow into the beautiful person our *Gardener* sees.

But grow in the grace and knowledge of our Lord and Savior,
Jesus Christ.
2 Peter 3:18

PETUNIA

The petunia is a genus of about 35 flowering plants native to South America. The plant is closely related to tobacco, tomatoes, potatoes and chili peppers.

SOMETHING FANCY

I took my daughter with me when I went to the nursery to pick out plants for the summer pots and flower beds. She was ooh-ing and ahh-ing over some large, gorgeous flowers while I was trying to decide how many petunias I needed for several containers on the deck. When I had a full flat of various colors, she joined me at the register.

"Oh, Mom," she exclaimed with disappointment in her voice. "Why didn't you get some of those fancy plants? You bought plain, old petunias?"

I thought about her statement as I planted the colorful plants the next day. Yes, they were plain old petunias. However, they would bloom all summer, they wouldn't need much care, they would thrive in the sunshine and they would grow rather quickly. I knew what those petunias would look like when they were in full bloom. They would be a beautiful addition to the deck and would bloom continuously.

There are times when the world might classify our lives as *plain*. But we can thrive wherever we are and bloom despite less than optimum circumstances. We can love the Lord, be willing to take on lowly tasks and do them without complaint. God knows what we do and the motivation in our hearts. He also knows the end result of our efforts can be stunningly beautiful even when it is done by plain old 'us.'

The Lord does not look at the things man looks at. Man looks at the outward appearance, but the Lord looks at the heart.
1 Samuel: 16:7

SUNFLOWER

There are over 60 varieties of sunflowers. They can grow from 3' to 10' tall with heads that measure 12" across and contain 1000 seeds.

TURN TO FOLLOW THE (SON)

The sunflower is very popular with photographers and artists. It has everything you could want in a picture: vibrant colors, simple, clean lines, and familiarity. Nearly everyone knows what a sunflower looks like and the many uses for the seeds. Some things you may not know about the sunflower are: the seeds aren't really seeds, but fruit and the plants are often used to absorb dangerous minerals from the ground, such as lead, uranium and arsenic.

Perhaps the most important fact about this flower is the reason they are called sunflowers. The heads always follow the sun. It doesn't matter where they are planted or which size or variety they are or if it is a single plant or an entire field; they lift their faces to follow the arc of the sun.

We humans come in all shapes and sizes, too. There are many things about us that our friends and relatives are familiar with, but we all have a few little known facts which only God knows. If we lift our faces to receive the warmth of our Heavenly Father's love each day, the light and warmth will enable us to face any and all problems we encounter and enjoy peace in his presence.

The Lord make his face shine on you and be gracious to you, the Lord turn his face toward you and give you peace.
Numbers 6:25-26

Surely then you will…lift up your face to God.
Job 22:26

ZINNIA

Zinnia varieties include both miniatures and giants which range from a foot tall to over three feet tall.

CHANGE OF OPINION

Zinnias originally grew as wildflowers, native to the southwest United States, Mexico and Central America. When Spanish explorers first saw the flowers, they thought they were ugly and named them, 'The Sickness of the Eye' or eyesores. Today, zinnias are one of the most popular, easy-to-grow, and most colorful flowers in any garden.

What changed? Time and attention was lavished on those perceived *eyesores* to develop them into the flowers we enjoy today. It took many years for researchers to change the zinnia's appearance and acceptance.

Our sins make us unattractive. We can be thankful when God looks at us, in our original state, he doesn't see us as eyesores. Instead he sees us as beautiful, useful beings who are redeemed by the blood of his son, Jesus. Just as zinnias attract butterflies, we attract people to our heavenly Father by our actions and our words.

The common zinnia of our gardens, Zinnia elegans, is also called youth-and-old-age. We need to take a lesson from this common flower; all people, of every age, are useful in God's kingdom. The next time you see a beautiful zinnia blooming, stop for a moment and remember they were once called eyesores.

....so that in every way they will make the teaching about God our Savior attractive.
Titus 2:10

ROSE

Whatever you're looking for in a flower—beautiful shape, lots of color, enchanting fragrance—can be found in roses. Rose gardens have been around for centuries and will remain with us for many future generations. Ancient Egyptians, Chinese, Greeks, and the Romans all grew and appreciated roses. Empress Josephine, Napoleon's wife, surrounded her palace with every variety of rose then available.

DANGEROUS BEAUTY

Immigrants to the New World often carried rose bushes with them, sometimes taking them to the far West in covered wagons.

I don't live in a palace and I didn't move to my present home in a covered wagon. However, every home in which I have lived had roses somewhere in the gardens. Roses are beautiful and seductive. Roses can also be dangerous if you get taken in by their charms. I have often ended up with scratched bleeding hands as I reached into the rose bush to cut the perfect blossom. Hidden beneath the beauty of the flowers are vicious thorns that can grab the unsuspecting hand.

The attractions of the world are like a beautiful rose garden. They're alluring and seductive, enticing us to try some of what is offered. But then the thorns of sin grab us and we find it hard to get away.

But we aren't hopelessly trapped. Jesus wore a crown of thorns as he died on the cross for all of our sins. Now we are free and assured of eternal life in heaven—a place a thousand times more beautiful than any earthly rose garden.

When you are tempted, he [God] will also provide a way out
so that you can stand up under it.
1 Corinthians 10:13

LAVENDER

Lavender is a species of aromatic herbs originally from the Mediterranean. The name is derived from the word lava, which originally referred to a torrential downpour of rain and then became the word lavare, "to wash." It alludes to the ancient custom of scenting bath water with oil of lavender or a few lavender flowers. That is still done today in the form of lavender bubble baths or body washes. Dried lavender is used as a sachet or potpourri.

PLEASING AROMA

At my former home, I planted a low lavender hedge along my driveway. Each time I walked by I would rub a leaf or one of the beautiful purple spikes to release the sweet, spicy aromatic oils that are in every part of the plant. On sunny days, I didn't even need to touch the plant to release the aroma—it filled the air.

We need to be more like the lavender plants. I'm not suggesting we dress in purple and stand in the sun giving off a pleasant aroma. But God does want us to be a pleasing aroma in the world. We are to spread the "fragrance" of Jesus' love and forgiveness to everyone we brush up against.

Our everyday actions are observed by others, leading them closer to God or away from him; however, like the lavender plant, we can *release* God's love to others without being asked or prompted or 'touched'.

"But thanks be to God, who always leads us in triumphal procession in Christ and through us spreads everywhere the fragrance of the knowledge of him [Christ]."
2 Corinthians 2:14.

BLEEDING HEART

The outstanding characteristic of bleeding hearts is the shape of the flowers. They are heart-shaped and a little "drop of blood" dangles at the bottom.

DISAPPEARING ACT

Bleeding hearts are traditional favorites in shade gardens. They bloom profusely in the spring with long branches covered with many, many bleeding hearts. They form large bushes with attractive fern-like foliage. However, all that foliage tends to die back after the plants are done flowering, leaving behind large empty spaces in the flower bed.

This plant does a great disappearing act once it's done blooming. If you didn't see the bleeding heart when it was blooming, you wouldn't know it was there. Unwary gardeners may destroy the roots in their eagerness to fill in the empty space by digging a hole for a new plant.

Unfortunately, sometimes our christian lives are similar. We are enthusiastically involved in teaching Sunday school, VBS, or helping with the Altar Guild. But then we get tired of doing the same thing over and over. We "drop out" and do a disappearing act. That's when we need to remember that Christ never disappears from our lives—we are always near and dear to his heart. "[Jesus said] I am with you always, to the end of the age." Matthew 28:20.

And let us not grow weary of doing good, for in due season
we will reap, if we do not give up.
Galatians 6:9

DAYLILY

There are hundreds of hybrids and cultivars covering a wide range of colors and sizes. Every part of the daylily is edible and may be added to salads or used as a garnish. The genus name for daylilies is Hemerocallis, from the Greek words meaning "day" and "beautiful". The flowers are beautiful but last only one day, being replaced by another bloom on the same stalk the next day.

CONSIDER THE LILIES

There are many, many colors and sizes of daylilies. The common orange one can be seen in vacant fields, along streams, and in roadside ditches. When I was growing up on a farm we called those orange daylilies "road lilies".

Perhaps Jesus was referring to daylilies when he talked about the "lilies of the field" in the Sermon on the Mount. Jesus reminded us that God takes care of the common flowers of the field by providing sunshine and rain so they can grow and flourish.

We are worth much more to God than a daylily so we can be assured that he will take care of us by giving us what we need. God loves us so much that he sent his son, Jesus, to die for our sins and give us eternal life. Nothing can be greater than that! What are you worried about? What is making you anxious? Give that worry and anxiety to God who cares for you.

Consider the lilies of the field, how they grow: they neither toil nor spin, yet I tell you, even Solomon in all his glory was not arrayed like one of these. If God so clothes the grass of the field, which today is alive and tomorrow is thrown into the oven, will he not much more clothe you?
Matthew 6:28-30

HYDRANGEA

Hydrangeas are an old-fashioned shrub famous for their large flower heads. They are native to southern and eastern Asia and the Americas, with the most varieties in China, Japan, and Korea.

ALL TOGETHER

I had a hedge of hydrangea plants, but they weren't all the same. Some were "mopheads" with large round flower heads resembling pom-poms or the head of a mop. The other variety was called lacecaps. These had flat flower heads with some flowers in the center surrounded by outer rings of showy flowers.

One thing both the mopheads and the lacecaps had in common was the flower heads were made up of many separate small flowers that combined to make one huge bloom. The small flowers by themselves were insignificant but together they made an impact.

Christians can be compared to the hydrangea. We can do God's work individually but when we work together with other Christians to spread the good news of salvation we make an even bigger impact. Paul speaks of that in Romans 15 when he says to live in harmony with each other to speak of Christ.

May the God of endurance and encouragement grant you to live in such harmony with one another, in accord with Christ Jesus, that together you may with one voice glorify the God and Father of our Lord Jesus Christ.
Romans 15:5, 6

IRIS

Iris is a flowering plant with showy flowers. It takes its name from the Greek word for rainbow, referring to the wide variety of flower colors found among the many species.

FLEUR-DE-LIS

The fleur-de-lis, a stylized iris, can be found in many coats of arms. It was used as the emblem of the House of Capet. It is associated with France as Louis VII, who adopted it as a symbol in the 12th Century. In medieval times, the fleur-de-lis of the coats of arms were displayed on a flag. This flag was carried before the army when they marched into battle and it served as an incentive as the soldiers fought for their king and country.

As christians we have a "banner" that we follow in our daily lives. It is the cross of Christ and all that it symbolizes— Christ's death for our sins and his resurrection. We don't march behind a flag but we do fight battles every day. We fight temptations from the devil, the world, and our own sinful self. We cannot win any of these battles without Christ. Follow Christ and the ultimate victory is eternal life.

The next time you sing or read the hymn "Onward Christian Soldiers" really think about the words.

Therefore take up the whole armor of God, that you may be able to withstand in the evil day, and having done all, to stand firm.
Ephesians 6:13

MARIGOLD

All but one of the many species of marigolds originates in the American tropics and subtropics. The flowers, usually yellow or orange, are often daisy-like.

DUST OF THE EARTH

The genus name of the marigold is *tagetes.* The genus name, referring to the marigold's habit of just popping up from seed, comes from Tages, an Etruscan deity, and grandson of Jupiter, who sprang from the plowed earth. It's interesting that such a common garden flower has such an exotic explanation for its name.

Our ancestor, Adam, also came from the dust of the earth. But he didn't just pop up from the ground. Adam was lovingly formed by our almighty God, the creator of all things. Adam was perfect—made in the image of God.

Because of sin, we are no longer perfect and we will die some day. Our bodies will eventually return to the dust of the earth, but if we accept Christ as our savior, our souls will go to heaven where we will live forever with perfect bodies.

Thank God for his wonderful creation of all things—including you.

So God created man in his own image, in the image of God he created him; male and female he created them. Then the Lord God formed the man of dust from the ground and breathed into his nostrils the breath of life, and the man became a living creature.

Genesis 1:27; 2:7

PANSY

There are a wide range of pansy flower colors and bi-colors including yellow, gold, orange, purple, violet, red, white, and even near-black. Pansies typically display large showy face markings.

HAPPY FACE

The name *pansy* comes from the French word *pensee* "thought", as the flower is regarded as a symbol of remembrance. The name "love in idleness" was meant to imply the image of a lover who spends all his time thinking of his beloved. Another name, "heart's-ease" came from the woman, Euphrasia, whose name in Greek signifies cheerfulness of mind.

When I see pansies for sale in early spring, I always buy a pot or two. They give *me* cheerfulness of mind and bring a smile to my face.

We should be like those pansies with their happy little faces. God didn't create us with automatic smiling faces like the pansies. But in Proverbs 15:13, God tells us how to have a happy face; "A glad heart makes a cheerful face."

When we remember God's many blessings we have a glad heart. That overflowing gladness will show on our face. Those around us will, in turn, feel happiness. It is sort of a "domino effect" spreading cheerfulness.

A joyful heart is good medicine, but a crushed spirit dries up the bones.
Proverbs 17:22

SHASTA DAISY

Shastas are a mainstay of the perennial border. They are tidy, well-behaved plants that require only a little attention to put on a delightful show of flowers for most of summer.

EVER EXPANDING

I like daisies and always want some in my flower gardens. When I was a new gardener, I bought six small Shasta daisy plants and placed them about two feet apart in a border. I planted some other perennials to fill in the space between the daisies. That first summer, the daisies flourished and the border was beautiful.

The next spring the daisies came up but they had expanded and were crowding out the other perennials. By the third year, I knew I had to do some serious revisions of that flower bed—the daisies had taken over! So the pruning began.

Sometimes our lives can become like my flower bed. Work, a hobby, sports, or even volunteering can take over our lives and crowd out other things. There is nothing bad about any of these things—they are all gifts from God. But when we become so involved and engrossed in these pursuits that we have less and less time for bible study, prayer, devotions, or helping others they become invasive and need to be "weeded out" or controlled.

With God's help, we can establish and maintain a good balance.

But seek first the kingdom of God and his righteousness,
and all these things will be added to you.
Matthew 6:33

TULIP

Tulips are invaluable for early spring color in mixed borders. These beloved bulbs offer a definite sign that winter is history, and spring is here to stay.

SURPRISE!

On a warm fall day, I took my first graders outside for their science lesson. We dug up a small area outside our classroom windows. Each child put a tulip bulb in the ground and covered it with dirt. I explained that the bulbs needed to be buried in the ground for them to grow. Fall turned to winter. Winter brought cold weather and lots of snow. The tulip bulbs were forgotten. Then the warm spring sun warmed the ground. The week before Easter, the children had a big surprise—some of the tulips were blooming!

It was a perfect lead-in to the story of Jesus' resurrection. The bulbs had looked dead and dried up when we planted them but now they were growing and blooming.

Because our Savior, Jesus, rose from the dead, all believers will also rise from the dead to live forever in heaven with our Lord. What a magnificent promise that our dead bodies will be resurrected into glorious heavenly bodies!

Jesus said to her, "I am the resurrection and the life. Whoever believes in me, though he die, yet shall he live."
John 11:25

CORAL BELLS

Coral bells are also known as alumroot. They are low-growing perennials that have thin, long stems with bell-like flowers along them.

DIFFERENT ROLES

Coral bell flowers grow on thin wiry stems in a variety of colors ranging from dark red, pink, and white. The flowers alone are not very impressive. But they grow from clumps or mounds of heart-shaped, boldly veined leaves. These beautiful leaves can range from very dark to radiantly silver.

Both parts of the plant need each other and have a role to play in the flower garden. Without the stems of bells waving in the breeze, the leaves may go unnoticed. And without the gorgeous leaves the flowers would fall over and be overlooked.

Like the coral bells, Christians have different roles in the church. Some of us are like the flowers calling attention to the gospel message with our witnessing. But we can't all be preachers or teachers. So others are like the beautiful leaves, grounding the coral bells. We use our gifts quietly by serving and supporting the work being done.

Now there are varieties of gifts, but the same Spirit; . . . All these [gifts] are empowered by one and the same Spirit, who apportions to each one individually as he wills.
1 Corinthians 12: 4,11

COREOPSIS

Coreopsis plants have daisy-like blooms in yellow, orange, or pink. The blooms are long- lasting, growing on carefree plants.

WORKHORSES

I always have several clumps of coreopsis in my flower beds. The plants have cheery yellow flowers that bloom all summer and attract butterflies. One flower catalog described them as "sunny flower border workhorses".

When I hear the word "workhorse" I have a mental picture of a large sturdily built animal. So that word may seem to be a strange way to talk about a delicate daisy-like flower. The writer was describing how the flower blooms all summer and never quits until frost kills it in late fall.

As Christians we can learn from the coreopsis. I don't mean that we will be delicate sunny people [which wouldn't be a bad thing] but that we will be workhorses. We can use the gifts and talents that God has given each of us to help others and to spread the good news of Christ's love and forgiveness. We can work for Christ and his kingdom all our lives until we die and are given eternal life in heaven.

And whatever you do, in word or deed, do everything in the name of the Lord Jesus, giving thanks to God the Father through him.
Colossians 3:17

DAFFODIL

Daffodils are trumpet-shaped perennial flowers that bloom from bulbs during the spring. Daffodil is the common name for a narcissus.

IT MEANS WHAT?

The ancient Greeks believed the daffodil flower (Narcissus flower) came from the self-centered Greek god, Narcissus. He was so egotistical that he fell in love with his own reflection in a pool. While looking, he fell into the pool and drowned. The Greeks said he was transformed into a daffodil (Narcissus) flower. So the daffodil is a symbol of unrequited love.

The daffodil is the national flower of Wales. In Wales it is said if you spot the first daffodil of the season, your year will be filled with wealth.

In Christianity, the daffodil along with the tulip is a symbol of Easter and the resurrection of Christ. The bulbs look dead when they're planted but in spring they pop up and bloom. Jesus was really dead when he was buried but he rose again on the third day.

Daffodils are considered to be one of the most popular, colorful and vigorous flowers of spring. In fact, the daffodil flowers are the first sign of spring. They show God's order and command of the natural world.

For everything there is a season, and a time for every matter under heaven.
Ecclesiastes 3:1

CARNATION

Carnations (dianthus) are flowering perennial plants that are often treated as annuals in cold climates. Carnations work well as cut flowers, in flower beds and borders.

LONG HISTORY

The carnation has a history that dates back more the 2,000 years and it was among one of the first plants to be cultivated in European gardens. In medieval times they were grown for their medicinal and flavoring properties as well as for their clove-like scent.

Carnations are still very popular today in gardens and as cut flowers. They can be seen in the lapels of a teenager escorting a prom date or the groomsmen in a wedding party.

Even though God's Word is a thousand times more important than any flower that God created, it could be compared to the carnation. God's Word has a long history beginning at creation when God spoke and the whole universe came into being.

The Bible reveals God's plan of salvation and how it was fulfilled with Christ's death and resurrection. It also tells us of God's love and care throughout our lives . . . from childhood to old age. The Bible assures us that when we die we will enter the glories of heaven where we will live forever with Jesus.

Your word is a lamp to my feet and a light to my path.
Psalm 119:1

BALLOON FLOWER

The balloon flower is a herbaceous perennial found in Japan and nearby parts of China. Summer is the main flowering time.

OPENING UP

Balloon flowers get their name from the unopened buds, which swell up prior to opening and resemble little hot-air balloons. Children are fascinated by these plants and like to 'pop' them by squeezing the sides, making them open with a soft, popping sound.

A clump of unopened balloon flower buds are not much to look at. They sort of resemble a balloon that has deflated. But once the buds open, the true beauty of the cup-like flowers can be seen and appreciated.

Sometimes we are like those unopened buds. Others can't tell what we are really like, what we think, and what we believe. People can get the wrong impression or no impression. When we "open up" to others, they can see Christ working in our lives through our actions and our words. In Matthew 5:16 Christ said, "Let your light shine before others, so that they may see your good works and give glory to your Father who is in heaven". Open up to those around you and tell them the good news of salvation.

You are the light of the world. . . . Nor do people light a lamp and put it under a basket, but on a stand, and it gives light to all in the house.
Matthew 5:14, 15

BABY'S BREATH

Baby's breath is a garden plant grown for its many tiny white flowers. Baby's breath plants have many-branched stems that bear numerous tiny white flowers about 1/8 of an inch wide. They are used in bouquets and grown in front of shrubbery in rock gardens.

SOFTENING TOUCH

As I hold my sleeping baby granddaughter, I can feel her soft wispy breath against my neck. One plant of the genus *Gypsophilia*, is commonly called baby's breath because it has a soft wispy character . . . like a baby's breath.

Almost everyone has given or received an arrangement of flowers from the florist that contained a few sprays of baby's breath. Because of its multitude of flowers, branches of baby's breath give an airy softening touch to bridal bouquets, corsages and boutonnieres.

We need to be like these flowers when we deal with our friends, coworkers, and neighbors. When we talk to others we need to use a soft approach, especially when we are witnessing to them about the saving message of the gospel. The "hard sell" seldom gets results. Instead we can relate to them in their everyday lives. Then when the opportunity arises, we can sincerely and gently talk about what Jesus means to us and our life.

Therefore, we are ambassadors for Christ, God making his appeal through us.
2 Corinthians 5:20

DAHLIA

Named after the Swedish botanist Dr. Andrew Dahl, the genus Dahlia, has around 30 tuberous-rooted species. They originated from Mexico and as far south as Colombia.

DIFFERENT—BUT THE SAME

Dahlias can range from huge, dinner plate-sized blooms down to midget pompoms only 2 inches in diameter. Dahlias grow from 1 to 5 feet tall and flowers come in every color except blue. The form of the flower is also varied from shaggy mops to peony-like and ball-shaped. They show as much diversity as any summer flowering plant.

But in many ways, dahlias are all the same in that they are immediately recognizable. They also have the same needs as far as water, soil, and sun are concerned.

People are somewhat like dahlias. We are immediately recognizable as humans even though we come in many different body types, skin coloring, and temperament. We speak a variety of languages, have numerous life styles, and originate from many ethnicities. But in the most important way we are all alike because we are all God's children.

God loves all people and sent his son, Jesus, to die for the sins of all. Forgiveness and salvation are offered to all people no matter how they look or where they live. Heaven will be filled with a wonderful variety of redeemed humans.

He [Jesus] is the propitiation for our sins, and not for ours only but also for the sins of the whole world.
1 John 2:2

AFRICAN VIOLET

African violets are native Tanzania and southeastern Kenya in eastern tropical Africa. Several of these native species are endangered because the cloud forest habitats are being cleared for agriculture.

FUSS BUDGETS

Both my mother and my mother-in-law loved African violets. Their homes were filled with these plants covered with flowers in shades of purple, pink, and blue. They made the care of African violets look easy, so I tried growing some of my own. Then I found out, through trial and error, that these houseplants are fuss budgets. They need just the right kind of light, temperature, and watering. Too much sunlight and they die, too high a temperature and they wither, and water on their fuzzy leaves kills the leaf and makes it drop off.

Sometimes we Christians can be fuss budgets, too. Someone says something that offends us and we are ready to cross that person off our "friend list". Or the people in the church don't seem as friendly and open as we would like them to be, so we decide we will go to a different church . . . or not at all.

We want things to be perfect in our relationships, but that won't happen because we are all sinners. That is why Jesus died—to forgive and save sinners. We need to do the same; be willing to forgive.

But I [Jesus] say to you, Do not resist the one who is evil. But if anyone slaps you on the right cheek, turn to him the other also.
Matthew 5:39

AZALEA

Azaleas are a flowering bush and foundation plant, with bright spring blooms. They are popular potted plants often given as gifts for Easter and Mother's Day.

THE RIGHT SOIL

Each spring, I have a bout of "azalea envy". As I drive around my town, I see large azalea bushes covered with beautiful flowers. Azaleas may grow wild in the Smoky Mountains and bloom like crazy in my neighborhood but they don't bloom by my front door. I have tried growing them but all I get are puny little bushes that don't flower and eventually die. I don't have the right kind soil to grow azalea bushes.

Jesus talked about various soils in his parable of the sower. The seeds fell on all types of soil but the only seeds that produced grain were those that fell on good soil. Jesus explained the parable by saying that the seed is the word of God. Some people hear the Word and don't understand it. Some are enthusiastic about the Word at first but fall away when trouble comes into their lives. Others hear the Word but the cares and pleasures of the world choke it out.

The seed sown on the good soil are the people who hear and understand the Word. They bear fruit by living a God-pleasing life and spreading the good news of salvation.

As for what was sown on good soil, this is the one who hears the word and understands it. He indeed bears fruit.
Matthew 13:23a

FUCHSIA

Fuchsias have exotic-looking flowers; their two-tone colors are brilliant.

SHADE LOVERS

Each spring, I buy a fuchsia plant. They are completely different from the other plants that I put in my garden and containers. Fuchsias are delicate looking plants; perfect for hanging baskets where their beautiful unusual flowers can trail over the edge. There is only one place in my yard where I can hang this plant; in a tree on the edge of the lawn. The fuchsia is perfectly happy in the shade protected from the hot sun. It blooms all summer, lighting up that corner of the garden.

Fuchsias can't survive the bright sunlight, scorching heat, or strong winds. They need protection to live and grow. We are like the fuchsia in that we need protection, too. We can withstand the sun, wind, and heat of summer, but we need protection from sin, death, and the devil. God is our protector who watches over us and cares for us.

God sent his son, Jesus, to die on the cross for our sins. Now we are forgiven and when we die we will live forever in heaven. Jesus defeated the devil and with God's help, we can resist the temptations of the world and the devil.

The Lord is your shade on your right hand. The sun shall not strike you by day.
Psalm 121:5, 6

MORNING GLORY

The morning glory, from Mexico and South America, is an annual climber with heart-shaped leaves. It has funnel shaped flowers that are usually sky blue.

SUN LOVERS

In my former home, I had a large back yard with a chain link fence surrounding it. Each spring I bought a few packages of morning glory seeds and planted them along one fence. Within a month the fence was covered with morning glory vines bearing hundreds of brilliant blue flowers. This fence was in full sun because these flowering vines need sunlight to thrive.

They are called morning glories because their trumpet shaped flowers unfurl with the morning sun and close up when the sun goes down. They hardly bloom at all on cloudy or rainy days.

We are like the morning glory because we also need the sun to survive. We need the earthly sun to be healthy and thrive but as christians we need the heavenly Son— Jesus. Jesus overcame sin, death, and the devil by his death and resurrection. Now we are forgiven and will live forever in heaven after we die. The morning glory follows the *sun* just as we need to follow the *Son*.

Again Jesus spoke to them, saying, "I am the light of the world. Whoever follows me will not walk in darkness, but will have the light of life".
John 8:12

LIATRIS

Liatris is also known as blazingstar or gayfeather. They bloom from late summer into early fall when the flower beds can use a shot of color.

NONCONFORMISTS

Liatris are unique garden flowers because of the way they bloom, from top to bottom. Blossoms first appear on the head of the flower spikes, and then begin blooming down its length to create a long fuzzy tube of purplish flowers. The top of the flower spike can be cut off and placed in a vase to enjoy and the rest of the spike will continue to bloom in the garden. These plants bloom in September when many of the other flowers have faded or died. Liatris are the nonconformists of the flower garden.

Maybe we should be more like the liatris, showing nonconformity in our lives. I am not talking about having wildly colored hair and extreme-looking clothes. And I'm not suggesting that we live in a cabin in the woods with no modern conveniences. We need to be nonconformists in our daily lives as christians. When we have Christ in our lives, others should notice that we are different in our words and actions—we don't conform to the world.

Do not be conformed to this world, but be transformed by the renewal of your mind, that by testing you may discern what is the will of God, what is good and acceptable and perfect.
Romans 12:2

DELPHINIUM

The genus of this plant comes from the Greek word for "dolphin" because of the shape of a gland in the blossoms that secretes nectar.

THE "LOOK AT ME" FLOWER

With their gorgeous spikes of jewel-like shades of blue, lavender and glowing white, delphiniums seem to say, "Look at me. I am the greatest flower in the garden." Some varieties grow up to five feet tall. Delphiniums certainly do stand out.

But there is a dark side to this towering beauty. All parts of the delphinium plant are poisonous and could be fatal.

While describing the delphinium, I thought of Jesus' parable of the Pharisee and the tax-collector praying in the temple. The Pharisee bragged about how good he was and all the wonderful things he did. He stood in a prominent place in the temple so everyone could see and hear him. Back in the corner where he was not seen, the tax-collector bowed his head and prayed, "God be merciful to me, a sinner."

The delphinium is us when we don't actually pray; only boast and want people to "look at us." Our words are poisonous to our spiritual life. We should strive to be like the tax-collector who knew he was sinful and needed God's forgiveness.

Everyone who exalts himself will be humbled, but the one who humbles himself will be exalted.
Luke 18:14

ASTER

Asters are part of ancient Greek myths. Asters were believed to repel snakes and were an antidote for snake venom.

LATE BLOOMER

Gardeners favor asters because they come in a variety of colors and are easy to grow. Asters are often a prime target for birds, bees and butterflies because they are fragrant and colorful. Asters are late bloomers, doing their best in the fall—right up to a freezing frost. When so many other flowers are at the end of their growing season, asters continue to thrive and provide brilliant color and sweet scent to a somewhat dreary sad landscape.

Where are you in the "seasons" of your life? Perhaps you are in the autumn of your life and things seem rather old and dreary. When you feel that way, remember that God is with you through all the years of your life. Jesus died for the sins of all people, no matter how old they are.

There are no age limitations on how long we can serve God by leading a christian life. We are never too old to tell others the Good News of salvation or pray for others. We can be late bloomers and still spread the beauty of God's love and forgiveness.

Young men and maidens together, old men and children! Let them praise the name of the LORD, for his name alone is exalted; his majesty is above earth and heaven.
Psalm148:12, 13

HIBISCUS

Hibiscus plants are tropical shrubs that have beautiful flowers that range from 2 inches to 1 foot in size. The flowers are bell shaped and appear in a wide range of colors but usually only last for one day.

SEVERE PRUNING

One summer I had a gorgeous hibiscus that lived on my sunny front porch. Before the first frost, I brought my hibiscus indoors and placed it in a sunny corner. As time passed, the flowers got smaller and smaller and then there were no flowers at all and the leaves were dropping off. By the next spring there were mainly bare stems with a few leaves clinging to them.

I gave the plant a severe pruning and put it in a sunny place outdoors. After a month of rain, sunshine, and fresh air the plant recovered and had shiny green leaves and several flower buds. By summer, it was its former gorgeous self.

Our christian lives are sometimes like my hibiscus plant. Our faith needs regular feeding and the stimulation found in bible reading and study, prayer and church attendance. When we deny ourselves this spiritual food, our faith shrinks and dries up. Occasionally God needs to give us a severe pruning to cut out unhealthy habits and ideas so the gospel message can make an impact in our lives.

Every branch in me (Jesus) that does not bear fruit he takes away and every branch that does bear fruit, he prunes, that it may bear more fruit.
John 15:2

We sincerely hope you have enjoyed these 50 devotions. Perhaps you learned some 'flower' facts you didn't previously know. We certainly did as we researched each one.

Our intent as we wrote these devotions was to present the gospel of Jesus Christ in a beautiful, common way just as God created beautiful, common flowers for our enjoyment.

If you would like to contact either of us to comment or you are in need of a speaker or would be interested in having this book available for sale in your place of business, you can reach us by e-mail:

gloriadotywriter@gmail.com
Jeanette.dall@comcast.net

Copyright 2015

Made in the USA
Charleston, SC
15 April 2015